LOVE ISN'T LINEAR

A COLLECTION OF POEMS
BY
SARA SALAM

Acknowledgements
I am grateful to the individuals - family, friends, and strangers - who inspired the content in these pages. Thank you for the insights that sparked these words.

Author portrait photographed by Christina Wehbe

All rights reserved. No part of this book may be used or reproduced in any manner whatsoever without written permission, except in the case of brief quotations embodied in critical articles and reviews.

ISBN 978-1-7337263-1-3 (pbk.)

© 2020 Sara Salam

 www.sarasalam.co

 @bysarasalam

For those who
love
without condition

ALSO BY SARA SALAM

My Truth Journal
www.mytruthjournal.com

LOVE ISN'T LINEAR

A COLLECTION OF POEMS
BY
SARA SALAM

The Peacock Pen Press
2020

CONTENTS

Introduction..1

Time..3
Bad Dreams...5
Consumed..6
It's Complicated..7
This Way...8
Love's Inferno...9
Classic Male Panic..10
Compassion..11
Summer Love...12
14 Things I Loathe About You...............................13
Love Making...14
Zero to 100..15
Denial...16
Someone Like Me..17
Shannon..18
Forbidden Love...19
Handmade Hearts..20
Mama..21
The Archer..22
Freed..23
Leave Me Alone..24
Stealing Love...25
Because You Lived...26
My First Christmas Without You..........................27
Let It Rise..28
Me..30
Love Isn't Linear..31

About The Author...33

INTRODUCTION

This book of love is not about the fairytales. It is a book about Love's fragility, it's fatefulness and fleeting nature.

This collection is a tribute to the raw feelings we endure, in happiness and in despair, in hope and in fear, in strength and in struggle that take over our senses when we experience one or more of Love's many layers.

It is through these seasons of life, the light and the dark, that Love presents itself.

For embedded in Love's many forms - romantic love, familial love, friendship, loss, compassion and self-love - we find sources of own our truth.

This journey is neither direct nor straightforward. The order of the works included in this collection reflect this reality.

May you always have the courage to speak your truth, and love without reservation.

TIME

We shared time, we shared space,
take me back to the place where
we grew up together, when there was no
    time to waste.
Oh, how could you go ahead and replace,
    me.

She said, our time has passed,
There's nothing but gilded glory,
a remnant of the past.
Who wants that? A tribute to sorry,
I no longer need you?
Breathe. I'm not the girl you once knew.

I am me, I am hope, I am truth, love and
    wonder.
So you are, I see too, even though you chose
    the lightning and the thunder.

He said, our time is now,
There's so much power in our story,
rooted in the past.
I want that, a tribute to glory,
I still need you.
Breathe. I'm not the boy you once knew.

I am me. I am hope, truth, strength and heart.

So you are, I see too, even though you are
        tearing us apart.

We shared fears, we shared dreams –
but now, it's not what it seems,
this life, this love,
this quilted, cool chaos,
ripping at the seams.
Oh, sweet soul, I love you, but this drama,
        it schemes me.
Breathe. We are not the peace we used to be.

BAD DREAMS

Sleepless, shapeless
Nights that creep tasteless
into our lives
sultry and chasteless.
Speak to me, you dark angel,
cunning and faceless.

A spirit that hovers, lurks
haunting, harrowed, weightless,
screams silent, no fear,
punctuated by a braised kiss,
Sing to me, you tempt'uous devil,
beguiling and fateless.

Dreams, may they come,
swiftly and angstless
into our sleeps,
soulful and sanctless.
Pray for me, you hopeful human,
may your armored heart be gateless.

CONSUMED

Consumed –

Am I doomed?

Holding onto a version of you

I've created in my mind.

Am I blind?

I see, with hope, a happy ending.

Could it be?

Or is it a dream –

made real only by the life I give it.

Can this happily ever after exist?

IT'S COMPLICATED

Together yet apart,
this game of dueling hearts
prompts a tacit affair
filled with whimsical, wild dares.

In our damnation,
we found commiseration.
I fell for you,
that's the truth.

I don't know where that leaves us.
Tonight, I grieve us.
Whatever it was –
A just because?
A parenthesis –
A breath of bliss –

Feelings unreturned.
Will I ever learn...

THIS WAY

That California beach,
within Heaven's reach,
shores of sand beneath our wandering bare
      feet.

Your presence is so calming,
like bay breeze on Miami mornings,
the sonorous sound of two hearts –
      in harmony, they beat.

So when I'm deep, in sleep, where my dreams paint pictures of you,
I see our memories play back in a catch-22.
When time stands still, and we kiss without
      shame -
I will always treasure us this way.

Kindreds sharing life,
exploring dark and light,
we laugh in bliss and take our pains in stride.
But all I really know,
You need space to heal and grow,
But I'm glad we both feel safe when we
      confide.

When you find my eyes, I smile in surprise,
I will always treasure us this way.

LOVE'S INFERNO

Pitchforks and halos
fiery with Agni's flow –
Emotions ablaze, caught tangled between
     hate and hope.

I love you, I loathe you,
I miss you, I chose you,
My insides wage war for peace beyond you.

Troubled, yearning,
desperate, discerning,
Despite my internal fire, simmering,
     burning –

Heated with heartache,
warmed by tender taste,
My flames dance in a tango of frenzy and
     Fate.

CLASSIC MALE PANIC

Manly yet manic.
It's classic male panic –
your actions and feelings often deserting yet
    volcanic.

Some days you'd hold me,
Other days, you'd disown me.
On no days was ever "I love you" told to me.

I should've known,
but I've grown,
I hope you're happy with your icy, Italian
    throne.

COMPASSION

We all suffer.
Have you ever wondered
what enters the minds of your friends and
    brothers,
who cry in the night
yet love you despite
all their pangs and problems that abuse their
    insides?

We all share
feelings of despair,
caused by the shadow side of Life's inky heir.
Choose compassion and love,
the world needs more because
we all deserve to feel the hand of God's
    gracious glove.

SUMMER LOVE

We used to dance and sing all day,
a couple kids making waves and catching
      rays.
cruising down the beach in your swanky
      Ford,
belting out tunes – "whatchu waiting
      fooorrrrr"?

You had your surfboard, I had my shades,
the setting sun closed out our days.
We chased hope like Obama preached
out here, holding hands, on the beach.

WHAT I LOATHE ABOUT YOU

I loathe the way you talk to me,
And the way you swivel your chair.
I loathe the way you type and click,
I loathe it when you stare.

I loathe your big dumb standing desk
And the way you take your calls.
I loathe the way you make me think,
It drives me up a wall.

I loathe the way you always smile,
I loathe it when you're high.
I loathe it when you make dumb jokes,
I loathe it when you make me cry.

I loathe it when you make a point,
And the fact that you speak in drawl.
But mostly, I don't loathe you,
Not even your haircut,
not even your love of bobblehead dolls.

LOVE MAKING

Shimmer and sway,
You shine bright today.

A metallic sheen of glitter and glow,
Your breath heaves gently in ebb and flow.

Howl and rage –
Your peaks engage –

Fighting furious under the sun's blister
Climaxed by a calm, sealed by a whisper.

ZERO TO 100

Our love was fast, our dreams were bold,
We pursued our stars, and truth be told –
I wouldn't change a thing, despite our
    parting
when you said that you couldn't give your
    heart to me.

Your courage to love led to your leaving.
You opened yourself, but at the same time,
    deceived me.
Zero to 100, that's what you said
to me when I asked what was going on in
    your head.

"I love you," you said, "it's just not the right
    time.
I need to find myself and clear my mind.
Maybe one day it will work out between us,
I'm just not ready to be what you need, love."

And so we moved on and out of our chapter,
You, to Chinatown, and me, ever the adapter,
found solace and comfort in myself and my
    home,
Two years gone by, and I'm loving me on my
    Own.

DENIAL

I made him smile.
Do I feign denial
chasing a life of bliss
which includes his kiss?
A question that haunts me
as much as it daunts me.

SOMEONE LIKE ME

You need someone like me,
Quiet yet free,
to love you like you always dreamed you
    could be.

I need someone like you,
Solemn and true,
to honor my soul and heal what's bruised.

We need each other,
as friends and lovers
to dream our big dreams and encourage one
    another.

Meet me here,
at the corner of Hope and Fear,
where we started our journey over two
    Helmsman beers.

SHANNON

You call when you need me,
I do the same.
We've shared memories, meals,
and 8-claps during football games.
Unconditional, our friendship
has seen 12 years of adventures and dreams,
Friends are family you choose,
I'm glad you chose me.

FORBIDDEN LOVE

We were peers, just friends
who shared stories as if time would never end.
At first, on a team tasked with building a map,
We worked one on one, line by line, bitmap by bitmap.
And then, something changed when we spent time alone,
innocent enough, two human beings
Bonding – then torn.

Both humbled and broken, time made us this way.
After months of torrid love, this is the price we pay.
You changed me, for the better, I'm a new version of me.
I am stronger, I am awakened, I am proud, I am free.
I don't regret these choices we made,
I will cherish you in my memory, until my memory fades.

HANDMADE HEARTS

Throwing darts
at handmade hearts,
making love as shadows that dance in the
      dark.

I see you, in the light,
that betrays your secrets of pain tonight.

You hear me, through the sounds,
in stories of truth that write this town.

We seek solace and comfort, a friendship so
      new –
a reminder that love can be forsaken yet true.

MAMA

On Friday nights, we dance, drink and disco –
    round and round,
Calling Baton Rouge, we make Garth proud.
We enjoy Taco Tuesdays and happy hour at
    Newport Landing,
Not to mention Gulf Stream's smoked
    salmon and crisp martinis.
We share our love of romance and works of
    smart fiction,
But what I love most is how you always
    listen –
To my stories, my pains, my rambling rappés,
Your patience is an orchid that blooms for
    days.
You are the keeper of my secrets, my light
    when it's dark,
I hope that you know, from the bottom of my
    heart,
From now, until Time decides it must end,
I am so lucky I get to call you my best friend.

THE ARCHER

I thought we'd be friends,
but this is where it ends.
No more bosom buddy benefits and marital
    sins.
These feelings, they're sharper
in the wake of your (most recent) departure.
I deserve better from you, you wandering
    archer.

FREED

I used to cower in your shadow,
Fearing your scorn, I had to lie low.
Despite this fear, I knew I loved you.
It tore me up, you were my boo.

Still, I am torn,
feeling sad and scorned.
Where does the soul go, that seeks to be
　　　reborn?

And so I freed myself, I walked away –
in truth, I didn't think you'd ask me to stay.
I was a mystery, a secret, a fantasy untapped,
but now I'm the woman you couldn't redact.

I moved on, I entered a new phase of life,
of courage, of strength, of consummate light.
I feel no shame for the time we shared,
but our time has passed,
　　　it's my time now, my savoir-faire.

LEAVE ME ALONE

Long ago, we loved as kids.
Eighteen years later,
You're making another bid.
It's over, it's done,
You're not the one.
Stop trying to be my anachronistic pun.

STEALING LOVE

Rainy days
and cabernet
keep hooded heartaches so stealthy in play.
Stealing kisses,
strawberry wishes,
masked as flavored love – savory and
      delicious.
And so you stole.
Now I know:
Love is rock'n'roll for your gypsy soul.

Rhythmic and blue,
for all I knew,
You were tempo'd and timeless, electric and
      cool.
I watched you go,
for all I know,
You found new love while dancing alone
to that Madonna track,
a two-note flashback
reminds me how our future was hijacked
by your wafty ways,
your nomadic gaze,
while I find myself missing you, I'm glad you
      didn't stay.

BECAUSE YOU LIVED

I still cry, by myself, all alone, in the car,
while I drive, speeding home, as light
      becomes dark.
My tears, mostly joy, for the time that we had,
Other times, though, I cry because I'm hurt; I
      feel empty, I feel sad.

Post-loss me, tired yet free,
Can't you see,
how you haunt me, your love, how it honed
      me,
But I know it was time...
And now it is mine, my time to shine.

I still write, all the time, any chance I get,
Committing words, thoughts, dreams so I
      won't forget
my tears, my loves, my pains, my woes,
Drafting pages of personal proverbs that
      chronicle my growth.

I still smile, by myself, all alone, in the car,
while I drive, sailing home, as memories fill
      my heart.
My tears, mostly joy, for the time that we had,
Other times, though, I cry because I'm
grateful, because you lived –
      lived a meaningful life as my dad.

MY FIRST CHRISTMAS WITHOUT YOU

So close and yet so far,
I see your face smiling back on our Christmas card.
Little time has passed, yet I'm living in a different world
absent of your presence, your laugh, your wisdom pearls.

I'm happy, you see, living the life you always wanted for me,
Chasing dreams I wish you were here to see.
I believe in my heart it was your time to go,
as much as I accept it, my heart still broke.

I miss you everyday, and I will for as long as I live,
Know I carry you with me, because in me, you live.

ME

I've always admired pieces of people,
Zalina's fashion sense, Nadine's sex appeal.
On some level, I knew I was different,
Petulant, impatient, perhaps a little
    irreverent.

For this reason, early on I accepted myself,
as a girl who swings to the knell of her own
    bell.
I journey through life loving all of me
for my visions of freedom, all I can and will
    be.

Call me selfish, independent, elusive, or vain –
I love who I love, including me, without
    shame.
I have lessons to learn and new adventures to
    find,
opening my heart and exercising my mind.

I own who I am, and so, you see,
The only person I ever wanted to be, is me.

LET IT RISE

Waves crash unchaperoned.
Thrashing, savage, grieving, they moan –
I gaze silent, a witness to this dance in ire,
a stormy, black match of pithy, wet fire.

I feel my soul burn, it churns,
rapping in motion that mimics the ocean,
I feel sadness, a suffering, a delicate
        uncertainty,
a light in my soul that yearns to be free.

Let it rise, let it fly,
can't hide in fear anymore.
Let it rise, let it fly,
in chasing my dreams, I soar.
I am free and I'm finding my way,
Let the waves rage on,
the surf screams and shouts in vain anyway.

Don't be afraid, you have what it takes,
to fight, to survive, to shape your own fate.
Over the moon and across the world,
Your courage sparks the spirit in that
        inimitable girl.

Let it rise, let it fly,
I grow as I spread my wings.
Let it rise, let it fly,

My roots ground me as I pursue my dreams.
Here I go, and here I'll stay.
Let the waves rage on.

My words, they compel strong emotion and
    thoughts,
they prompt introspection, deep feelings –
    cold and hot.
My words provoke awareness, acceptance,
    and appreciation,
for all that we are as this life's creation.

LOVE ISN'T LINEAR

Laughter lit up by almond champagne,
Stealing kisses by moonlight on the
    Champs-Elysees.
Cherub cheeks flushed with pinkness after
    Baby first wakes,
Tear-stained eyes marred by heartbreak
    when Daddy climbed Heaven's
    staircase.

Up and down, over and above,
My heart rises and falls with the seasons of
    love.
Sometimes smiling, sometimes full,
    sometimes heavy and hard –
I breathe in the moments that bring light to
    my dark.

Though love salutes strength and courage to
    feel,
It can surrender to pain when it doesn't know
    what is real.
Hearts filled with hope outlive minds filled
    with fear,
Please remember, my darling, love isn't
    linear.

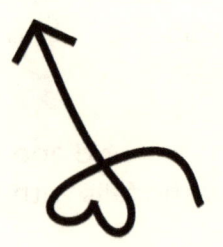

ABOUT THE AUTHOR

Sara is an award-winning author and editor. Published since age 11, her writings range across young adult fiction and nonfiction, poetry, movie reviews, newspaper and magazine articles, blog entries, and a guided journal. Sara resides in Southern California where she enjoys writing, yoga and the beach.

www.ingramcontent.com/pod-product-compliance
Lightning Source LLC
Chambersburg PA
CBHW021134080526
44587CB00012B/1283